Eight Hurricane Maria Stories from Puerto Rico

Robert Egan

ISBN: 1983782564
ISBN-13: 978-1983782565

In Memory of Salvador "Chan" Solís León
(1924 - 2017)

ACKNOWLEDGMENTS

Thanks to Lilliana and her family for just about everything. Thanks to my own family for helping us purchase a generator and to Isaac for shipping it here. Thanks to Ony for letting me drive a bulldozer. Also, thanks to you for reading.

CONTENTS

SHOULD I STAY OR SHOULD I GO?

"Should I stay or should I go?" More and more people who feel stuck in storm-ravaged Puerto Rico are asking themselves this very question.

This question is also a song by The Clash.

While tuning in for answers, I notice all of the backup vocals are in (bad) Spanish.

The Clash collaborated on this song with a musician from Texas. Supposedly, spur of the moment, they decided to do the backup vocals in Spanish. One of The Clash's singers knew a bit of Castilian Spanish, the musician from Texas knew some Tex-Mex, and one of the sound engineers called his family members to help with the translation. By one account, this sound engineer had family from Ecuador. According to another account, this sound engineer was Puerto Rican.

I live in Puerto Rico. I speak bad Spanish. I wonder whether I should go now, or stay to experience the aftermath of Hurricane Maria.

This 35 X 100 square mile island wasn't exactly in good shape before the storm hit. For years, the government has been accumulating high amounts of debt (over $72 billion to date), the outdated power grid has been deteriorating, and Puerto Ricans (especially young graduates) have been asking themselves "should I stay or should I go?" Many have left for the States, and it looks like there's another mass exodus in the works. Maria was the most powerful hurricane to make landfall here in over 80 years. Maria was the last thing this place needed, and it's probably going to get a lot worse.

So, maybe I should... Split!

Before I settle on an answer, I should probably tell you what brought me here in the first place.

The streets of Berlin are responsible.

It's summer 2015. I've been living in Serbia off and on for a couple of years and decide to take a trip to Switzerland then Germany with my best friend from Belgrade.

In Berlin (our last stop), I'm searching for a parade. People have told me that this parade is coming back for the first time since 2010. This event used to be called the Love Parade, and it started shortly after the fall of the Berlin Wall. A caravan of trucks, held together by the willing masses, would play electronic music and blast its way through a reunited Berlin. The Love Parade spread throughout Germany until millions would take part in it each year.

Then in 2010 in Duisburg city, the Love Parade went wrong. Near a tunnel entrance to the festival, overcrowding set off a panic. Over 20 people were trampled to death as others made their escape, and the Love Parade was permanently canceled. Now, it's being brought back in 2015 under a different name, the Train of Love, and promises to be smaller (about 50,000 people instead of several million).

The Train of Love is taking place on my last full day in Berlin, but I can't find an exact address. Out of three possible locations, I choose the one that appears most often. My friend doesn't want to join, so I explore the empty streets lined by ornate but tasteful architecture on my own. After a couple miles of this sedate scenery, my hope is dwindling.

Then, I hear it: UMP-kzzz UMP-kzzz UMP-kzzz UMP-kzzz.

An army waits in ambush around the corner. I wolf down some sausage and sauerkraut at a food cart, then enlist.

Thousands upon thousands of us slide down the avenues at a groovy pace, conquering all with our sound. Rather than keep a steady beat, the dozens of music trucks bend time. You can speed up or slow down to march behind a truck of your choosing, passing through worlds where a rhythm lasts a lifetime and a note merges past existences with future reincarnations in the blink of an eye.

My favorite truck has a couple of bald, bearded old guys balancing big beer bottles on top of their domes and dancing to the accompaniment of electric violins.

At strategic moments, smaller bands detach from the main company and swarm like locusts through grocery stores and gas stations to collect and redistribute good German beer (all German beer is good). I stock up on beer several times but don't know if I've been marching for minutes or days.

Resurfacing between waves of sound, I see that the Train of Love is passing by my hostel block. I tear myself away from the procession and go looking for my friend. Sure enough, he's standing outside the entrance smoking cigarettes. I try to convince him to join the parade.

During our back and forth, I notice a girl seated nearby on the hostel stairs. She has curly black hair that glows like a red halo under the Germanic glare of the sun. Big mirrored lenses cover her eyes, the right lens falling an inch short of a beauty mark on her cheek. I guess that she's from somewhere in South America, and her head is halfway tilted towards our conversation. She looks like she's waiting for someone.

I pretend she's waiting for me.

"Would you like to join us for the parade?" I ask.

"We're waiting for friends," she says, carefully. We talk with her a bit more, and I find out she's from Puerto Rico. A group of noisy British tourists who look like they're fresh out of high school burst out of the hostel doors. They give us the briefest of glances before continuing on their way.

"Okay, let's go," she says and stands (I don't ask about the 'friends' but learn later that she was referring to the British tourists who all but ignored us for whatever reason and whom she had met only minutes ago). My friend, the girl, and I venture into the parade and let it carry us down the avenue.

Farther down the boulevard, she and I squeeze into a gas station to find more beer while my friend waits outside. People inside have picked the place apart, but she snatches four big bottles ahead of others' grasping fingertips, shoves aside useless dairy products in the refrigerated aisle to make room for the beer, keeps our chilling spoils of war safe on all sides while we wait in line, then offers to pay. Later, she asks for my help with finishing one of her beers. She might be the woman of my dreams.

Shortly after the beer, my friend bids us goodbye for the day (he told me later that a big strong hand groped his buttock while he was waiting for us outside. This made him rather uncomfortable, since his reason for not wanting to join the Train of Love with me was he was convinced it was a gay parade).

Left alone, my and her conversation travels in ever tighter spirals, as if we're both afraid to come to a full stop in the center. We walk from side to side, then up and down the cars that form the Train of Love. Finally, in the tired twilight of a city that's seen so much, the parade comes to a halt, and so must we.

The crowd spreads out but at least one truck is still playing. It has changed its tune from inexorable electronica to something slower and more melodic. We dance.

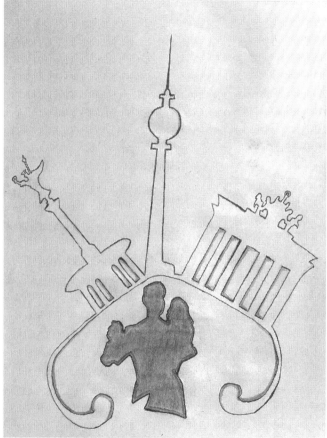

I'm not sure if we're dancing Salsa or the Waltz. I don't know how to dance either one, so I just spin her around a lot. She protests when my hand drops lower than her waist, so I kiss her instead. We stop in the middle of crosswalks to build on that first kiss. It takes us hours to get back to the hostel.

The next morning, we say goodbye in the hostel lobby. She tells me to consider visiting her, and I promise to do just that.

The magnitude of my mistake doesn't hit me until I'm in the airport with my friend. He turns to me and says, "You know you could've at least been a gentleman and bought some damn internet to exchange contact details with her." (The hostel we stayed at in Berlin was silly in a number of ways, one of them being you had to go to the front desk to purchase internet access by the hour).

She and I didn't exchange any concrete contact information.

I rip my computer out of my bag and wrack my brain for details. I know her first name (but not the spelling), and I know her last initial. She's a classical musician and was taking a short trip to Berlin from Austria, since she's there for a summer program. I remember the program is more about opera singers than the musicians and that the city in Austria sounds like the way Italians say 'thanks.'

That should be enough: How to say thanks in Italian → Grazie, Austria → Did you mean Graz, Austria? → Graz international singers program summer 2015 → AIMS festival → orchestra roster. In about ten minutes, I have her name.

I'm lucky that there weren't more twists or turns. Also, the girl may've not been much help on her end (she confessed later that she thought my name was Kevin and worried it would have been rude to ask again).

I visit her in Graz, then she changes her return ticket back to Puerto Rico so she can visit me in Belgrade. Many of our pictures from that time contain an obtrusive but ever-friendly blob (a piece of German kebab that found its way into her camera shutter).

From there, I visit her in Puerto Rico once, then twice. The third time, I pack what I can into one duffle bag, bring my dog, and move to San Juan in mid 2016.

There you have it: love brought me to Puerto Rico.

So, should I stay here for love? That's a loaded question, but if love traps you in one place against your will and keeps you from making healthy decisions, then it's no longer love.

In the dark early weeks after Maria, my girlfriend told me she'd understand if I needed to leave for a few months to keep up with my online work and to recuperate. And I could. She has more attachments in Puerto Rico that would make her leaving more complicated, but she can take care of herself and has wonderful family and friends who would be there for her. Unless that offer was her tricky way of trying to get rid of me, I would say the love is still there and it has grown.

There has to be something else to keep me in Puerto Rico.

Should I stay here because I have nowhere else to go? That is the grim reality for many people on the island. When Maria obliterated the power grid, many parts of Puerto Rico were thrown back into the 18th century. The sad part is that the ones who may really need to leave the island have less of a chance of doing so. They may live in remote mountainous regions where clean drinking water is a distant daydream. They may have a family member with a life-threatening illness who can no longer find proper treatment in Puerto Rico's crippled hospitals. They may not be able to afford plane tickets, whose prices skyrocketed after the storm. To put it bluntly, they are poor, and they are being left behind.

I'm fortunate that leaving is an actual option for me. Every time I talk with my mom, she imagines this scenario where I, my girlfriend, and my dog come to Tennessee and live with her and my dad until the situation in Puerto Rico magically gets better. Their house has plenty of room, and my girlfriend's family is invited.

So if I can go, should I stay in Puerto Rico out of shame? There has been some backlash against people who appear to have left the island so easily. Many of those who have made their escape are wealthy. Once they're safe in the States, they suddenly become more patriotic and talk about raising awareness. Sometimes, I suspect that they just couldn't live without air conditioning. Still, searching for my own reason for staying or leaving is difficult enough without guessing at the substance of another person's being.

You're reading this collection of stories because I found my reason. I realized there was something else besides love that brought me to Puerto Rico. It has taken me many places, and it feels like destiny with a touch of free will. Without it, you can't be in love or feel alive.

I'm staying in Puerto Rico for adventure.

Adventure doesn't have to be exciting at every turn. Sometimes, it's simply accepting a challenge then seeing it through day by day. Like a good story, it should feel surprising yet inevitable.

When I made the decision to stay, I believed it would, hopefully, be a once-in-a-lifetime experience. I thought this adventure would last a few weeks at the most. As I write this, our neighborhood has been without power for over two months. During those roughly eight weeks, eight stories took shape. You've just finished the first, and seven more await you. Some are longer. Some are shorter. Most are non-fiction, but I promise to throw a few curveballs your way. Enjoy, and may adventure find you when you least expect it.

RIDERS ON THE STORM

Maria was supposed to be my rebound hurricane after Irma.

I was here when Puerto Rico braced itself for Irma on September 6th. That category 5 wreaked havoc across the Caribbean before battering herself senseless against Florida. Along the way, she was supposed to pass through Puerto Rico, and I was excited for the new experience.

My girlfriend Lilliana insisted that we ride out Irma with her folks in the mountains of Guaynabo. While I really like her family, I found this arrangement disappointing. Our apartment in San Juan is so close to the ocean that you might be able to hold your breath and walk to the nearest beach (if you can hold your breath for about two minutes while crossing four lanes of traffic). So, by heading to Guaynabo, we were getting farther away from the action.

In the days leading up to that storm, I heard doomsday predictions about how Irma would knock Puerto Rico and its crumbling power grid back into the Stone Age.

That didn't happen.

As Irma made her approach, we spent the early evening watching *Makkhi*, a Bollywood movie about a man who reincarnates as a housefly and learns how to kill bad guys to protect his one true love. The winds in Guaynabo picked up enough to knock out the power, and we didn't get to finish *Makkhi*. I joined Lilliana's father on their barred-in porch to watch the breeze rattle the trees. Showers of leaves and branches splattered the streets, but I wanted to see a tree shoot past us like some giant squid soaring through the storm. I waited to no avail then went to sleep.

Irma had changed her mind at the last moment. She'd bent her path around the island and let out a few farts on Puerto Rico's shores before turning her malevolence elsewhere. The local papers praised the Puerto Rican government's organized response.

There were clean-up crews on Guaynabo's streets before sunrise. The especially rapid response there was probably due to the city's new mayor wanting to prove his mettle. He was voted into office during a special election to replace the previous 5-time mayor, who resigned due to scandal. Throughout his reign, the old mayor had covered the city's roads in roundabouts. There's a monument in the center of each one. These monuments range from something that looks like grasshoppers mating to a victory shrine honoring cockfighting legends (cockfighting is legal in Puerto Rico) – kind of a strange legacy for the old mayor to leave behind (unless he was using the traffic circles and their art to launder money). Anyway, all the roundabouts plus monuments that I could see in Guaynabo had weathered the storm just fine.

In our neck of the woods, the power outage was more an inconvenience than a calamity. The power in the metropolitan area tends to go out after a heavy rain, and we'd already experienced half a dozen blackouts in our San Juan neighborhood before Irma. This was nothing new.

Overall, the island got lucky. The governor Ricky

Rosselló declared disaster for some areas, like Vieques and Culebra (two tiny islands off Puerto Rico's east coast), and about 1 million people across Puerto Rico lost power, but Irma's aftermath was a lot less worse than many had anticipated. Less than a week after the storm, Puerto Rico was in good enough shape to provide refuge for and deliver aid to people from the nearby islands.

As events failed to diverge from normal, I felt cheated by this happy ending. I know it's sick of me to say so, but I had wanted to see more destruction.

Had I been expecting a post-apocalyptic wasteland, some place where I'd wield a machete and hunt iguanas with my dog before defeating Don Sluglord in the slime pits and returning to everyday life? Not exactly, but I had wanted something different, something more catastrophic.

About two weeks after Irma's passing, Hurricane Maria tore across the Atlantic. Dire warnings circulated once more as Maria made her way toward Puerto Rico. I told Lilliana about my disappointment with Irma, so she said that I should pick where we'd stay for Maria. I declared that we would remain in our San Juan apartment, right next to the mighty ocean.

Lilliana purchased a battery-powered radio, found a battery pack for her cell phone, cooked all of our frozen fish (then threw it away for fear of food poisoning), and bustled about in a flurry of pre-Maria activity.

My own preparations were less enthusiastic. I thought about getting plywood and nailing it to the outside of our windows then settled for covering the windows and balcony doors in crisscrossing masking tape instead (to theoretically keep the glass from shattering). We had enough canned food and water, so I was more concerned with trying to get as much online work done as possible before the next blackout, and with convincing my little dog to empty his bowels before we had to shut ourselves inside.

Halfhearted or not, all of those preparations wore me out by the night of the 19th. Maria was expected to make landfall around 8 AM on the 20th, so I planned to get a good night's sleep then see what she had to offer. Before we settled down in the dark, I took one last precaution.

Our apartment is on the second floor of an old but sturdy building, and we have a narrow balcony from which you can see a thin strip of sea. But when you venture out onto the balcony, that blue band of the Atlantic will not be the first thing you notice.

No, your first sight will be cables upon cables with the occasional power line thrown into the mix. As a conservative estimate, there are about 20 cables out there that twist and slant like mangled piano wires. All of these black lines are tethered to a crooked utility pole near the balcony's left-hand corner.

Despite my low expectations for Maria, I realized that wind plus water could be a dangerous combination if any of those lines ripped free and were somehow still live during the storm. I imagined water seeping under the balcony doors and across our floors, a puddle waiting to be pierced by a crackling cable.

I tucked a towel under the outward-opening balcony doors, tied my belt around the knob, and wrapped the other end of the belt around the leg of our kitchen table. By pulling on the other end of the table, I could hopefully keep the door pulled shut if it came to that. This last preparation was the most memorable for me, since it meant admitting that Maria might not be just another Irma.

We slept on an air mattress in our apartment's back room, or at least I slept. At 2 or 3 in the morning, Lilliana woke me up by fluttering a folding fan in my face, almost close enough to scrape my nose. The temperature had risen by about 10 degrees, and I was covered in sweat.

"It's coming," she said. The winds outside did sound louder than they had during Irma, as if an opera singer were humming a strange lullaby. I figured that difference in noise level was all down to the acoustics in our apartment building – it was simply a neat vibrato that was in no way menacing.

"No, it's too early. We should sleep." I followed my own advice.

She woke me the next time by shaking me. The battery-powered radio was spitting out frantic Spanish, and the opera hum had turned into a demonic whine. Something clanged against metal outside our apartment window.

"That's the laundry room roof. Something big is falling on the roof!"

"It just sounds big. Probably only a little tree branch

or some scattered pebbles banging against the sheet metal." Even though the clamor outside sounded like two fully-armored knights fighting one another with sledgehammers, I really believed my own claim in that moment. Maria wasn't supposed to come until later in the morning, so jumping at every little noise and losing sleep seemed unnecessary.

I kept slipping in and out of consciousness while Lilliana huddled over the radio with a lantern at her side. I had reached that state of deep sleep that most people hope to achieve on long-haul flights. Come to think of it my ears kept popping, as if we were in an airplane.

Broom. Bassoon. Baboon. Bathroom. Yes, bathroom. My girlfriend was saying we should head to the bathroom, the rearmost room in the apartment. Fine, anything to keep sleeping.

Before getting to the bathroom, I noticed the balcony doors were thumping against their frames. I pulled on the kitchen table that I'd lashed to the door knob with the belt. The doors quieted down. After congratulating myself for being a genius, I passed out on the yoga mat that Lilliana had spread across the bathroom tiles.

The doors started thumping again. Somehow, this sound bothered me more than the demonic chorus of winds or the battle sounds of metal bashing against metal. The gale outside was disrespecting my knob-belt-table invention: my knobeltable. I left the bathroom to work the knobeltable again, but the doors wouldn't stop thumping for more than a few seconds. When I pulled harder, the knobeltable tugged back. When I let go, it jerked across the floor in fits and starts until the doors resumed their knocking.

For the first time, I looked past my misshapen masking tape asterisks and the balcony door windows. A roaring wall of water encompassed the balcony. I say wall because there was no end to this continuous cascade. The water looked white to me, but I couldn't tell if this was the water frothing against the glass, the moon somehow shining through the storm, the faint light of first dawn creeping over the horizon, or a combination of all three.

Beyond this blast of white, I saw the shadow of a leviathan slithering through the night. This beast was too big for my mind to comprehend, so I focused on the parts closest to my end.

Black whiskers twitched against the glass, as if they already knew of my presence.

I backed away from the knobeltable and into the hallway leading to the bathroom, then stopped. I kept expecting whatever was out there to open its eye and tear our flimsy doors off their hinges. I couldn't feel fear. I couldn't feel courage. Those ideas were tied to everyday life, to the human realm, and whatever was out there couldn't care about feelings. The doors thudded in time to my retreating footsteps.

Maria was ahead of schedule, and all I could feel was dismissed.

Holing up in the bathroom no longer seemed silly. Lilliana was in there with the radio, which supplied nothing but static, and my dog Crusty was curled up near the base of the toilet.

"Stay awake!" Lilliana warned.

Of course. Of course. *Por supuesto*. I promised that I wouldn't go back to sleep, but now that I was in the middle of my first real hurricane, I didn't know what to do. I had heard all I could hear. I had seen all I could see. There was nothing I could do if Maria decided to claim our windows and doors. There was nothing left to do except to... sleep.

I awoke sprawled across the bathroom floor. Crusty sat at attention, staring at me reproachfully, but Lilliana was gone. My first thought was that she had abandoned me in the bathroom, but that was quickly replaced by panic: Maria had eaten my girlfriend!

I stumbled down the hallway and found her mopping the floor in the main room. The sun had risen enough for us to see, and the water had come in under our front door and the balcony doors. I helped out with some towels as we tried to recount what had happened. I praised Crusty for his bravery (he hadn't shaken once during the storm), until I found the brown puddle of diarrhea that he'd left in the corner.

Maria had passed, for the most part. When I poked my head out the door to throw Crusty's bagged-up poo outside for later, the sky was a gray-white purgatory. I walked out and marveled at the streaks of green that marred the white walls and red floors. Any leaves and branches that had found their way into the stairwell had been pulverized against the stone. A gust of wind knocked me off balance, so I crept back inside.

That day was a waiting game. I convinced myself that the black leviathan whiskers that I'd seen pressing against our doors had merely been the cables in front of our balcony. Most of those cables were miraculously intact, but a few trailed down to the street below. When Crusty let out another round of diarrhea, I tried not to compare it with some of our canned food. By the time I threw out this poop bag, the winds had lost some of their staying power. I went to investigate what had been the source of that clamor outside our bedroom window.

Maria had torn a sheet-metal roof free from the neighboring apartment building's penthouse. That awning had fallen four stories before smacking into our building's first-floor laundry room roof. The first impact must've taken out the laundry room roof instantly; it hung like a guillotine over the washer and dryer. The noises we'd heard, the noises that I'd nonchalantly told Lilliana were falling pebbles, were probably caused by the two roofs pummeling each other throughout the maelstrom until they found their final resting places.

Before Crusty could foul up the floor again, I took him on a walk up and down the stairs. Despite my best efforts, Crusty wouldn't pee or poop outside any of the apartment doors. Eventually, Lilliana joined us.

We climbed to the top floor and tried to survey the damage to the surrounding neighborhood. I saw that a few houses on our block were missing parts of their roofs, but the overall picture was hazy for me. We couldn't see much beyond our alleyway, and Lilliana shouted at me to get away from the railing whenever the winds picked up suddenly.

The apartment door on the top floor opened. Crusty immediately ran inside, lifted his leg, and peed on an overturned dog kennel top. I would have tried to clean up his piddle, but the entire floor was already soaked. Our neighbor and her snow-white dog were inside. She had stayed to watch over this apartment, which she and her husband used as a music school, while her husband had looked after their penthouse above. I gathered that they had had a worse time of it with flooding during the storm. Our neighbor looked dazed, and I made a stupid joke about having slept through most of the storm. I didn't know what else to say, so I held my squirming dog while she and Lilliana exchanged details and offered reassurances.

Back in our apartment, we learned from the radio that there was an island-wide curfew set for 6 PM, effective immediately. After sunset, the world beyond our apartment went pitch black. We tried to contact loved ones with limited success then drifted into dreams in a futile attempt to fill the empty silence left behind by Maria.

The next morning Crusty, Lilliana, and I went for a walk around the neighborhood and a nearby lagoon.

Most of the sidewalks were impassable, but the streets were devoid of cars. We walked around the fallen trees and crumpled metal, occasionally taking photos for evidence.

The Yam Burger, an open-air restaurant one building over from our apartment, looked like a partially gutted fish, with its metal roof tiles flapping and falling like so many discarded scales and its innards spilling out into the parking lot beyond. A mechanic's shop located farther back in that lot had at least a dozen cars buried under hundreds and hundreds of pounds of rusted sheet metal.

Closer to our neighborhood's lagoon, a huge green highway sign had blown apart into fragments. Part of it curled around a stone bench like a piece of parchment. Another section had severed some mangrove tree roots before getting stuck near the water's edge. A port-a-potty was lodged in this same collection of mangroves. I started imagining that all this had been the work of kids who had taken a neighborhood prank too far.

Lilliana stared at me, and I realized that I had been snapping photos and grinning.

Our neighborhood's section of Ponce de León avenue was a ghost town. All of the businesses were boarded up, and people scurried across the streets in small groups. A room in the building right across the street from us was missing an entire wall; it looked like a twisted diorama, some elementary student's idea of a broken home.

The days that followed were a lost time. I recognized that people must have died during Maria, but it wouldn't stop there. Despite being part of the U.S., it wasn't as if volunteers could hop in their cars and drive across state lines to deliver aid. It wasn't as if ships from nearby nations would be able to bypass bureaucratic barriers and provide supplies directly to the people. It wasn't as if all the hospitals, pharmacies, and supermarkets had somehow been left untouched by Maria's wrath. It wasn't as if the island's economy and infrastructure had been in anything resembling good shape before the storm. More people were going to die in the slow aftermath.

I watched Lilliana's face when she wasn't able to get through to her family in Guaynabo. I listened when she explained how we'd get past the roadblocks by biking a dozen miles to her family's house while carrying supplies and the dog. I felt the seconds and hours slip by as we tried to clean up our corner of the neighborhood and give ourselves a sense of purpose.

And what small part did I have to play in all of this? I had whined about not seeing a big enough storm, separated Lilliana from her family during a bigger storm, slept through most of that storm, then marveled at the destruction.

And that destruction. It looked like God had flown into a rage while putting together a jigsaw puzzle.

It looked like Maria had been the real deal.

It looked like a misbegotten wish.

EXECUTIVE OFFER

Howdy, *Amigo*.

My name is not important. Call me the voice above. With all the planes and helicopters buzzing overhead, some of the true patriots will be dropping my truth, my leaflets, my truthlets to float down to you folk. If you have the blessed fortune to be holding this sheet of paper in your hands, then you're on the final stretch. Read on to find out how you can make a difference.

You may know the big man, *el jefe naranja*, paid your island a visit. That much is true. But the mainstream media always got to put a spin on things. If the mainstream media had been around when Jesus-our-lord-and-savior walked this Earth, they'd say he was the leader of some cannibalistic cult. So... it should come as no surprise that those smoothie-sipping, scum-sucking journalists skipped the most important part of the president's visit to Puerto Rico.

Sure, they covered that neat scene where he threw paper towel rolls at all you excited natives in the church. And the cameras captured *el presidente* letting your governor Ricky sit on his right side and patting that nervous boy's hand. Hell, *el hombre con manos enormes* even congratulated all the agencies on a job well done before the real work could get into full swing. Generous. Compassionate. Congratulatory. A shining example of the commander-in-chief in action.

But the journalists got to turn every story into a smoothie. They take a great man's words, put them into a blender, and hit spin to get their next headline. Here is what the president said word-for-word:

"Every death is a horror, but if you look at a real catastrophe like Katrina, and you look at the tremendous – hundreds and hundreds and hundreds of people that died – and you look at what happened here with really a storm that was just totally overpowering, nobody's ever seen anything like this. And what is – what is your death count as of this moment? 17? 16 people certified. 16 people versus in the thousands. Uh, you can be very proud of all of your people, all of our people, working together. 16 versus literally thousands of people."

Now look at how the headlines twisted his words:
*President Says Hurricane Maria Was Not 'a Real Catastrophe Like Hurricane Katrina'
*President Says Puerto Rico Should Be Proud of Hurricane Death Toll
*Puerto Rico: President Compares Maria and Katrina Deaths

Listen, over 1800 people died because Hurricane Katrina hit America. For the sake of math, let's say that 18 of you people died because Hurricane Maria hit Puerto Rico. If you want to play that death count comparison game, then you could say that Puerto Ricans are 100 times stronger than the average American. Of course, the president, *el jefe que caga oro*, knows that NO ONE is stronger than the average American. Therefore, he could not have been making such a comparison at that time.

See? Simple logic is all it takes to defeat the mainstream media. Don't believe their lies. Don't even try to debate them. Two words is all they deserve: ¡FAKE NEWS!

Now that we're on the same page, let's get the story straight. The big man was not downplaying deaths and leaving your island to rot. No, he wanted to make Puerto Rico a deal, but he knew that he couldn't trust the dishonest media to tell you about it.

That's where I come in, *compañeros*. I am the president's strong teeth, his wise tongue, his stern but sensual lips. Here is the deal that none of the major news outlets are covering. This executive offer comes direct to you from *el hombre con la boca hermosa*:

Tired of being a second-class citizen with no voting rights in a government of the people, by the people, for the people... except for you people? Then this offer is for you, Puerto Rico! For the month of October only, as part of ongoing relief efforts in the wake of Hurricane Maria, you'll now be able to vote for three assistance packages with your lives[1]:

Hurricane Maria Level (10+ deaths): a free financial lecture and paper towel rolls thrown at your face (you're welcome)

Hurricane Ike Level (100+ deaths): a two-week business course that covers how to clear fallen forests to make way for golf resorts

Hurricane Katrina Level (1000+ deaths): a power grid that works some of the time and 15 minutes of national news coverage (commercial breaks included)

But wait, there's more. Die in the next 48 hours, and you'll receive an all-expenses-paid trip to Mar-a-Lagoooo,[2] regardless of total death count![3]

¡Vaya con Dios!

[1] Applicants who don't speak good American and who don't agree that this is the greatest deal ever will not receive a vote. The president is the greatest dealmaker of all time. He has the best words.

[2] Must use back entrance.

[3] Your death must be deemed to be hurricane-related and will be evaluated on a case-by-case basis. Any and all restrictions apply. Cases open to consideration include, but are not limited to, death due to downed power lines; lack of adequate medical care for cancer, advanced diabetes, heart conditions, etc.; generator fires, explosions, and carbon monoxide fumes; flooding, absence of clean drinking water, and waterborne diseases (including leptospirosis); heat exhaustion from waiting in lines; being out after curfew; gunfights over gasoline and/or gasoline containers; falling bridges, trees, and/or coconuts; angry women named Maria; and a hopeless bleak despair that tracks you in the darkness and seeps into your soul, and which cannot stem from the fear of being forgotten (for in that fear, there would still be hope) but must be borne by the realization that your death counts more than your life ever could.

THE TRIUMPH OF BUTT PANTS MAN

Today marks the month-long anniversary of Puerto Rico's whirlwind encounter with Hurricane Maria. 30 days with no power for most of the island, including our building and neighborhood. The scene that stands out the most to me so far is one that I didn't see in action.

This scene has to do with a well-known homeless guy who sleeps on the sidewalk outside the Banco Popular – he lies directly on the asphalt with no possessions in sight. He could be in his late 40s or early 60s, never asks for stuff from passerby, and frequently smokes scavenged cigarettes. Come to think of it, I've never actually seen him eat or drink anything.

I think of him as the BP man.

During the dusk before the storm, I was walking my dog one last time before we had to hole up in our apartment.

The BP man was in his usual place, not moving despite the sporadic gusts of wind. He seemed to have grown roots that had penetrated into the very sidewalk. I thought about calling out to him, but what would I say? Excuse me sir, but did you know there's a storm coming? Would you care to do whatever it is you do here at our place for the next 24-48 hours?

So I passed by without a word or gesture.

Not knowing what to say or do wasn't the only reason for my reluctance to interact with the BP man. I don't think of him as the BP man because he sleeps outside of the Banco Popular every night – that's just a coincidence. No, the real reason for this name is his trademark Butt Pants.

When he's on the sidewalk below, the Pants look tattered but relatively normal. But if the BP man stands up, and if you're anywhere in the 270-degree arc that fans out behind him, you will witness the Butt Pants. There really is no back to his trousers except around the waist and ankles. Depending on what he's wearing underneath, you'll get different phases of the moon. Definitely more than one full moon per month.

In the weeks after Maria, there were lines everywhere. Lines in front of gas stations. Lines in front of grocery stores. Lines in front of big hotels, like the Marriott, that had provided "community centers" for the public to charge their electronics (I waited in that line a lot to try to keep up with my online job, but they shut it down a couple weeks after the storm – if Marriott were a man, he'd probably give a dollar to someone on the street once then brag about his sense of charity to his business associates for the rest of his life). And yes, there were long lines in front of ATMs, including the BP man's Banco Popular.

I wasn't in the ATM line on the day that someone tried to take away the BP man's Butt Pants, but my girlfriend was. Here's the scene that's lodged itself in my head without my ever having seen it:

There are actually two lines to the Banco Popular: one for the ATM and one for wire transfers. The BP man lies in the midst of all these newcomers, yet he is unperturbed by their presence. Feeling the urge to stand and stretch, he uproots himself from the asphalt.

People avert their eyes but stand their ground. The lines hold.

Within minutes, several well-meaning federal aid workers approach the BP man. One of them carries a pair of crisp new pants. They wave the opaque fabric at various heights and angles as if it's a wondrous invention. They engage with the BP man, but he's not enthusiastic about their offer. The lines of people wait and hope.

So what if it's just a pair of pants? This clothing of the BP man, this eclipse of the unpalatable, could be a milestone along Puerto Rico's road to recovery.

Finally, the aid personnel convince the BP man to leave the premises with them. He's still wearing his Butt Pants, but his unsightly apparel will soon be erased from memory. The crowd heaves a collective sigh of relief. Some are on the verge of celebration.

Five minutes later, the BP man returns alone to Banco Popular. He's still wearing the Butt Pants. The new pants are nowhere in sight.

He sits back down in his appointed spot and remains there long after the disappointed lines have dwindled away.

Pride. Mental illness. A bit of both. Those are easy explanations for why the BP man rejected the new pants. A more interesting theory is that he needs the Butt Pants to survive. Maybe his backside is covered in microscopic but sturdy roots. Stronger than adamantium, these roots kept him firmly attached to the Banco Popular sidewalk while Hurricane Maria roared past. This would also explain why I've never seen him eat or drink anything – the roots allow him to absorb minerals and nutrients from the ground. He's the next step in our evolution, a completely self-sufficient human being. The one catch is he needs to wear the Butt Pants at all times to ensure direct contact.

The only information I have that might counteract this theory is I saw him at the grocery store on October 11th. The BP man had been waiting outside the store doors for something but had grown impatient. He strolled into the store and made a quarter turn among the waiting lines. A manager immediately arrived to assist him. Still, I don't know what he wanted to buy and have no evidence that any food or drink exchanged hands.

The lines in Puerto Rico continue to evolve, and we're fortunate to be in the metro area (most of the lines here at least have something on the other end). So, the next time you find yourself waiting for something you once took for granted, look for unusual details. Think of the BP man and his strange steadfast resolve. I know that I do, and in doing so, I'm convinced that most people will find a way to manage.

FIVE SURVIVAL TIPS

We've made it past week five without power in our part of Puerto Rico. Now I could bore you with advice about how to safely purify water with bleach, how to make coffee with prayer candles, or how to check whether a standing body of water is electrified, but those are disconnected bits of information that don't look beyond narrow scenarios. Life is a complex series of interwoven components, a sum that is greater than its parts. True survival tips must follow the very arrangement that makes life possible. They must work together to tell a story.

So, here's a handful of survival tips to celebrate week five:

#1 *Be positive.* If there is nothing positive in your life, try multiplying a negative by a negative.

#2 *Drink free water from the ocean.* Don't waste your money on water from the stores. After starting this new hydration technique, blisters may form around your general mouth region and the edges of your world could take on a fuzzy tinge. Don't worry! Those are just the toxins (found in bottled water) leaving your body. When in doubt, refer back to survival tip #1.

Robert Egan

#3 *To check for propane tank leakage, crouch down right next to the tank's nozzle and light a cigarette.* Okay, you're positive and hydrated, but you're worried that your propane tank might have sprung a leak? No problem. Inhale that lit cigarette deeply (really getting that ember glowing will also provide light if you have none), then blow the smoke over the nozzle. If the smoke swirls but does not waver, then you're all clear. Don't hog this survival tip all to yourself. Drag the propane tank outside and share this knowledge with your neighbors, the ones who possess the Generator from Hell. They'll be amazed by the results!

#4 *If you need a small favor from your neighbors, make the request memorable.* Before going further, I need to provide a little background on an object of ever-increasing importance in Puerto Rico: the generator. Many people complain about the sound and smell of generators. A lot of those complaints are frivolous and motivated by envy. We don't have a generator for our place yet, but why should I hate on a neighbor who had the finance and foresight to look out for their own best interests? I can stick to that line of reasoning with normal generators from this mortal realm. I can pretend that their steady hum speaks to human perseverance.

#4a But there is one generator that deserves no forgiveness. It is the Generator from Hell. It rumbles and sputters in the alleyway outside the basement of a business directly across from our apartment. Since Hurricane Irma (the one right before Maria), the people who own this business have taken up residence there, probably because their condo outlawed the Generator from Hell long ago. At first, I had warm feelings toward them. In the early weeks, they let me charge my computer several times and once gave me a shot of mamajuana (a liquor mix from the Dominican

Republic). I would have refused if I'd known the expectations behind these casual acts of kindness.

#4b The Generator from Hell runs from about 10 in the morning until 2 at night, and it's three times as loud as generators more than twice its size. Whenever it rains, the neighbors put a metal roof on top of the generator, and it sounds like bikers are having an orgy in the alleyway. The Generator from Hell also has a strategic placement. This means that its butt hole/exhaust port is right next to the gate of our rented parking space. Whenever I open the gate, the Generator from Hell spews carbon monoxide in my face.

#4c I have not borne this in silence. I have been, am, and will be positive; I drink more than 7 liters of ocean water a day now; and I have shared the propane tank tip with the neighbors not once but thrice. The neighbors have no appreciation for survival, and they have trouble with following basic requests. Listen to the Generator from Hell for too long, and you'll hear jazz saxophones bubbling up from the Underworld.

#4d I've decided to take a more memorable approach the next time I need to ask for a tiny favor (you will need a machete and must shout to be heard over the generator): "MIRA CABRÓN, I AM THE ETERNAL WIND THAT OUTLASTS ALL HURRICANES." (wave machete and make whooshing noise) "LOOK ME IN THE EYE WHEN I'M TALKING TO YOU." (tap the machete against your eye, or their eye – feel free to mix up the approach!) "PAY ME RESPECT OR I'LL TAKE IT FROM YOU... ALSO, COULD YOU TURN YOUR GENERATOR OFF AFTER 10:00 PM, POR FAVOR?" (jam machete in generator's butt hole and twist off the tip)

#5 *If you have a terrible secret from your past that may come back to haunt you* (e.g., a broken machete drenched in the lifeblood of the Generator From Hell), *then pack it up in a box and ship it to yourself through the USPS, FedEx, or UPS.* With the backlog of packages in Puerto Rico, it will never come back to you.

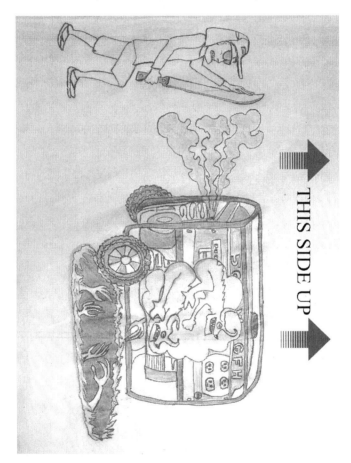

DEAD FISH

Nur tote Fische schwimmen mit dem Strom. "Only dead fish go with the flow." I don't know if this proverb finds its true origin in Germany, but I first saw it in German and enjoy how it sounds.

When coming up with this title, I hadn't realized that dead fish also fit well with the cancellation of the Whitefish contract. So, before we delve into this tale of passivity punctuated by promises of violence, let's get that coincidence out of the way.

Whitefish is a Montana company that has been around for about two years and supposedly had only two full-time employees when Hurricane Maria struck. The CEO of the company grew up in the same small town in Montana as the current Secretary of the Interior, and Whitefish was somehow able to secure a $300 million contract with the Puerto Rican power authority to repair parts of the power grid. Due to public outcry and federal scrutiny, that deal has recently found itself dead in the water.

So, after 45+ days with still no power for most of Puerto Rico, the restoration continues?

Anyway, the dead fish proverb also goes against another common saying: "Go with the flow." I like "go with the flow" about as much as "be in the moment." What moment? Whose flow? These sayings are half-assed attempts to control a person's sense of direction and perception of time. Instead, the dead fish proverb is about not being passive. It's about surviving and thriving despite the actions of others.

It's about not letting people take a dump on you.

In the story about survival tips, I tried to make light of an ongoing problem with our neighbors and their Generator from Hell (GFH). Here's the actual story with less attempts at humor.

These neighbors aren't full-time neighbors. Instead, they own a tailor's shop, a basement business whose service entrance opens into a 12-foot-wide alley. Our apartment balcony, directly across from the service entrance, is about 9 feet off of the ground.

For about six weeks, the tailor shop's Generator from Hell was chained up outside in the alley. It was running 7 days a week, 13-16 hours a day, and 15 feet (according to the Pythagorean theorem) from our balcony. Our bed is next to the balcony, so trying to get a good night's sleep meant either closing the windows to dampen the GFH's sound and smell while sweating it out, or incorporating its bodily functions into our nightmares. There were not many good nights.

Still, we probably could've handled that if it weren't for the space issue. We rent the driveway of a vacant house that's right next to the service entrance. Each time my girlfriend Lilliana parked, she had to worry about the generator scratching her car while the through traffic backing up behind wanted to barrel down the alley. Each time I bent down to unlock the gate, the GFH's exhaust port was a foot away and farting carbon monoxide in my face. Even when I was upright, I worried about the generator exploding and annihilating my crotch (the neighbors often let it run out of gas – we can hear the GFH's death clunks before they arrive soon after to pour more fuel into the already overheated engine).

So, why not just tell the neighbors to cut that shit out right now? The problem was one of hospitality. For the first couple weeks after Hurricane Maria, they let me charge my computer three times and gave me two shots of fairly good liquor (caña from Puerto Rico and mamajuana from the Dominican Republic). So, in return, I brought our neighbors bread from a nearby bakery, let them use our rented driveway twice, held off about complaining about the GFH's operating hours, and postponed making any requests about relocating that poorly placed generator. Five for five.

Thus, I went with their flow while my resentment grew. During one of my early conversations with the neighbors, the father (a slim man from the Dominican Republic in his late 60s) and the son (a hefty guy in his mid 30s with a big forehead) had claimed that they were turning the GFH off at 11 each night for the neighbors (not true, unless their clocks were set to Pacific Standard Time) and bragged about how they'd be getting a quieter generator soon.

About a week later, I was wringing out wet clothes off my balcony and watched while they unloaded a big red machine from a pickup truck. My hope died when I saw they were unloading a shiny washing machine instead of a generator.

By the fourth week, I started making polite requests. I told the son that we were having trouble sleeping and asked if they could turn the GFH off a little earlier. He said he'd see what he could do. When I suggested 10 PM, he offered to do it around midnight then changed the subject to how he's "fighting every day" to get by, like we're comrades-in-arms. Yeah right. I've been inside their well-insulated business while the GFH was running: it's as quiet as a cathedral and has air conditioning too.

That night, the generator did go off a little after midnight. The next morning, I saw the father. Instead of complaining, I thanked him for turning the generator off a little earlier, mentioned how we slept a little better, and emphasized how we'd appreciate it if it went off even earlier. I spoke in an mix of English and Spanish, and he replied in kind, but I wasn't sure if we understood one another. The following night, the GFH farted its way well past midnight.

We moved our bed to a more cramped back room, where we could still open a window and the noise was slightly more bearable (my girlfriend used noise-canceling earmuffs while I made strategic use of malt liquor). With the battle about operating hours at a standstill, I tried to focus on the space issue.

Whenever I heard someone setting up the generator in the late morning, I asked them to at least turn it 90 degrees to the wall. That would give my girlfriend's car slightly more clearance and point the GFH's butthole away from my face and into the alleyway instead. Most of the time, the son was the one setting up the generator. One time, he mentioned that the current placement of the generator was strategic then launched again into how he was "fighting every day," although he and his clothes looked relatively fresh. Lilliana came out and explained in Puerto Rican Spanish what needed to be done, and he begrudgingly acquiesced.

I asked them to relocate that generator three times, while still being friendly. Each time they moved it a little, but then... next day, same shit.

When I shared this story with a few others in Puerto Rico, I was hoping that it would help me feel better. But in talking then writing about it, I kept getting angrier. One friend told me his own generator story:

A neighbor in his building got a generator. The neighbor worked with him to soundproof the generator, then threw him an extension cord so he could have power whenever the generator was running. When that generator failed, another neighbor with a generator threw him a line. When more than one generator was running, the neighbors argued good-naturedly about who was going to supply him with power. They all chipped in on gas: Those were good neighbors.

This helped put my situation into perspective. During the first couple weeks, my temporary neighbors across the alleyway had put on appearances. They had said *mi casa es su casa* and told me that I could ask them for anything. This early kindness had charmed and disarmed me, but when I tentatively asked for the things that mattered, they couldn't be bothered. I was ashamed by how easily I'd been turned into a dead fish.

One day (when I wasn't there), they even had the nerve to use our rented driveway to wash one of their gas-guzzling SUVs. Lilliana came upon this scene and had to wait for them to back their ass out before she could park. She gave them a piece of her mind (politely), but nothing really changed.

More drastic action was required.

My original plan was to temporarily borrow (steal) three traffic cones, duck tape one to the building's drainage pipe, then duck tape the remaining two to the anchored traffic cone. This would help push the GFH aside and give us the necessary space that should have been respected from day one. I took my girlfriend out to dinner and halfway convinced her of this plan (by being a little vague about the number of cones required). There was a nearby street that was lined on both sides with traffic cones, but these were surprisingly well-guarded by a couple of night attendants. We scouted the street twice but had to return home empty-handed (I found out later that the street had been closed down for a film shoot).

One night later, we couldn't pull into the driveway because the GFH was in a particularly bad spot. It was crowned with a piece of sheet metal that further reduced our clearance. While the traffic backed up behind us, I got out of the car and moved the still running GFH, hoping that it wouldn't choose that moment to explode. I dragged the generator as far as its short chain would allow, so that it was close to the wall and partially blocked the back entrance. After we were parked, I retrieved a cheap red boogie board from storage and tied it to the building's rain pipe. My girlfriend wrote a message across the board in black sharpie (in Spanish):

"Please keep the generator close to the wall. Please. Thank you!"

Direct but still polite. The following morning, the boogie board with it message was still there for all to see. I heard the neighbors making more noise than usual while setting up the generator. By the time I got outside, they were gone... and so was the boogie board. The Generator from Hell was in a new place. The neighbors had drilled a couple of metal O-rings into the wall and chained the GFH to it. It was now at least 8 feet away from the driveway entrance, and the noise that reached our apartment was somewhat more manageable. I guess I should've counted that as a victory, but the missing boogie board bothered me.

Not that's not true. The boogie board's absence enraged me. I went to the business to get it back, but the father and son weren't there. I encountered the pair later when we were taking the car out of the driveway. They appeared uncomfortable. When the father shook my hand, I thanked him for moving the generator (and immediately lost respect for myself by doing so). When I asked about the boogie board in broken Spanish, the father's friendliness evaporated and the son looked like he was trying to stare me down. The father shook his head, and my girlfriend asked them in Spanish:

"Did you see the sign?"

"Yes."

"Did you take it?"

"No."

We exaggerated our movements getting out of the driveway, my girlfriend backing the car out to where their generator used to be, and I sticking my elbow and face into that infernal machine's former roost while closing and locking the gate.

After that encounter, something switched off in my brain. This missing boogie board was the last bit of disrespect that I could bear. Before that moment, I had been the good cop to my girlfriend's bad cop. We've since reversed roles. She still greets them and acknowledges their presence, but I refuse to interact with them. I have descended from friendliness into an explosive silence.

The son glares at me once when I'm on the balcony and he's setting up the GFH. I glare right back, but it's not enough. I want to leap down and show him what it means to be "fighting every day." With the father, I fantasize about verbal confrontations instead. I practice a few phrases over and over:

No son buenos vecinos. (You are not good neighbors.)

Esta no es tu calle. (This is not your street.)

No vives aquí. (You don't live here.)

The first couple times I cross paths with them, I whistle cheerfully, glance at them, then laugh. It may be my imagination, but I believe that both have taken to wearing these dark aviators more often. Once, I lock my eyes with the father's lenses while he's sitting with friends. We both nod slowly, like kung-fu masters bowing before the final battle.

Most of the time though, I just ignore them. They

don't try to say or do anything.

The new placement of the GFH is a relief, and they turn it off at midnight most nights now. I should be happy, but I can't let it go. For going on six weeks, they had been living in relative comfort while taking a dump on me and mine. And I took all that smiling. Lately, I have more energy, like I can run and never grow tired, like I can will mighty rivers to reverse course. It's intoxicating. It feels an awful lot like hate.

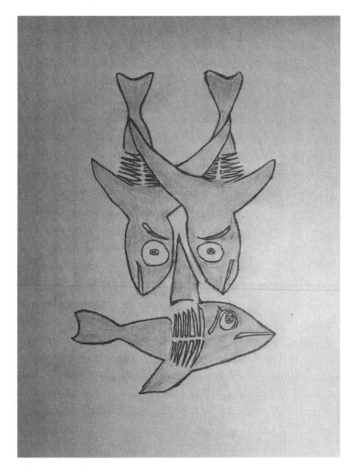

In the present, one wrong word, one wrong move, is all I need for this hatred to ignite into action.

If we lived in suburbia, it might be easier to sustain this silence. We'd each park our mid-sized sedans in our respective garages, walk into our separate homes to greet our 2.3 children whose future incomes will hopefully be greater than ours, and lose ourselves in front of flat-screen TVs that repackage the same ideas while promising us that we're part of something new. Checking the mailbox and mowing the lawn would be the only times we'd cross paths.

But I don't live in suburbia, and I don't want a TV. I cross paths with the father and son 3-4 times a day. These encounters are either in the alleyway or on the main street, while they're hanging out with other business owners.

I try to make a point of being friendly with everyone I encounter, except for them, especially when they're around to observe. I do my best to disregard their presence, but they and their past disrespect are always foremost in my mind. I must take deep breaths before I open the apartment building's gate, before our next silent encounter.

Several days after my boogie board went missing, I'm returning home from work. I usually work from home, but that's been more or less impossible (no power plus no internet at home for over six weeks now). After having security guards tell me to leave hotel lobbies and business owners let me know that paying $7 for a smoothie only gets me one hour's worth of time in their shop, I've found an office space that works most of the time and charges about $3/hour to be there, with mixed results.

Exiting the office space and worrying about whether I've worked enough, I notice that it's a beautiful day. Instead of reveling in it, I think about our neighbors and their Generator from Hell. This would be a perfect day to wash your car. Yeah, it would be a perfect day to wash one of your cars in a driveway that doesn't belong to you.

Sure enough, when I approach the apartment, the son is washing his car, except he's washing it on the main street. He's in no way, shape, or form invading our space. Still, the sight of him with that pressure washer, wasting all of that water and electricity, infuriates me.

In our driveway, near where the GFH used to make our inside and outside lives even more miserable than it does now, there's also a small garden. I have created and cared for this garden. I water the plants and try to coax clinging vines into interesting positions. I pretend I'm there endeavoring to cultivate my own garden, but I'm really hoping for a final confrontation with our unwelcome neighbors. I sweep up decayed leaves and litter, but I wish for violence.

Nothing happens, no one materializes in the alleyway, and I feel like I'm caught in that moment before a sneeze that will never come.

When I finally venture out of the driveway/garden, a red jeep flies through the alleyway but swerves in time to avoid hitting the Generator from Hell (if only there were justice in this world). I step back to keep from getting sideswiped and throw up my arms in disgust.

The jeep slams to a halt, its front tires skidding over the alleyway's small speed bump, the driver's side drawing level with my apartment building's gate. I walk around the back of the car and toward the driver's side to get to the gate.

"*¿Que quieres decir?*" (What do you want to say?) An unshaven man, about 40 years old and wearing a red baseball cap, leans out of the jeep's window and shouts at me. A woman, maybe his girlfriend or wife, sits in the passenger seat but doesn't say anything or look in my direction. Perhaps they have been having an argument about his driving, or he wants to impress her. Maybe he thinks I'm with FEMA. Whatever the reason, he's looking for a confrontation too.

"*¡Vivo aquí!*" (I live here). "Pay attention when you're driving."

"*No vives aquí. Vivo aquí. Habla en español cabrón.*" (You don't live here. I live here. Speak in Spanish, bastard.) He continues in a rapid fire mix of Spanish and a bit of English. I can't follow every word he says, but I get the gist of his argument:

1) Since I'm not fluent in Spanish, it's impossible that I live here.
2) People like me do not belong in Puerto Rico.
3) He, on the other hand, speaks Spanish and really is from Puerto Rico.
4) Therefore, I have no right to tell him to not run me over while he's driving.

Truly a master logician.

"*Debo practicar mi español para pendejos como tú.*" (I must practice my Spanish for assholes like you... my statement would have been more grammatically correct if I had used "por" instead of "para.") Rather than losing it, the man looks triumphant. I have acknowledged his irrational argument. He continues his lecture. I stop trying to follow a language that still eludes me and interrupt him in English.

"Okay. Teach me some Spanish. Step out of the car."

The man's words lose their rhythm. He imagined himself safe inside his metal cage, and the fact that I don't speak the language well seemed like an added bonus to him, but words will not help him here. I am in the street, his window is open, his door handle is nearly in reach, and the rear tires of his pitiful jeep haven't yet cleared the alleyway's speed bump.

For all intents and purposes, we are both outside.

I see this same realization dawn on his face. He inches his car over the speed bump.

"Step out of the car, or keep driving."

The man clears the speed bump and turns his head to say something more. This time, my Spanish is faster.

"¡PUTA!"

True to the name that I give him, he keeps driving.

Then, somehow, I'm back in the apartment. I'm trembling, but I feel powerful. I go for a run.

I suppose that I'm looking for that jeep, hoping to find its driver trapped at a traffic light. After remembering that most of the traffic lights in the area are no longer working, I dwell on my neighbors, the operators of the Generator from Hell. I hope to the place from whence their Goddamn machine came that they overheard the commotion in the alleyway. I want them to know that they are not welcome on my street.

I run all the way through Old San Juan, picking up the pace until canned food rises to the back of my throat. Willing the vomit down while trying to breathe is like losing a fight. I slow down to a steady pace, and my thoughts do the same.

So, what would've happened if that driver had stepped out of the car? I see three different scenarios:

1) We fight. One or both of us get injured. The hospitals are so backed up in Puerto Rico that getting any kind of medical attention that day would be unlikely, and I don't have health insurance. Plus, when someone (probably his passenger) calls the cops, the man can give them his own version of events in perfect Spanish while I struggle to string two sentences together.

2) He has a gun. Pop pop pop. There are no witnesses or cameras running in the alleyway. The red jeep drives away, and that stupid Generator from Hell is my last company on this Earth.

3) After I humiliate the man verbally then physically, he drives off with his tail between his legs. His hatred builds, and he remembers the very first words out of my mouth: I live here. He returns one day with friends and/or a weapon (although he'd first have to get over his earlier argument and admit, however indirectly, that someone like me does indeed live in Puerto Rico). If he doesn't have friends or a suitable weapon, then he could just run me down with his jeep. It wouldn't be particularly hard if I'm saddled down with groceries and walking my dog.

But the real question for me is this: If I was ready to go that far with a stranger in less than 60 seconds, then what's going to happen when I can no longer hold the silence with my neighbors of 6+ weeks?

When I tell Lilliana about what happened, she helps me visualize those different jeep scenarios and says that I should thank the neighbors for moving the GFH. I refuse, saying that we shouldn't have even had to ask and reiterating that they don't live here.

Still, that last part bothers me. *No vives aquí.* You don't live here. That was one of the Spanish phrases that I'd practiced, honing its edge for when I'd hurl it at our neighbors... but didn't the man driving the jeep say the exact same shit to me? That kind of argument is right up there with that nationalist nonsense that has reared its ugly head all across the States (by "all across," I don't mean only the South and rural areas: turning those places into easy targets is probably part of the problem).

I've lived in Puerto Rico a little over a year, and I want to tell people, whose shop has been here for a lot longer, where they do and don't belong? That's not right.

So what do I do? Is it turn the other cheek, or an eye for an eye? Do I want to be a dead fish, or a shark?

How about neither.

The next day, I encounter the father in the alleyway. I acknowledge his presence.

"*Buenas tardes.*" (Good afternoon). I hope my expression is neutral.

"*¿Todo bien?*" (Is everything okay?) He extends his hand. After a moment, I take it. Suddenly, he's warm and friendly again. He explains how he hadn't known about the space issue with the Generator from Hell.

This claim of ignorance angers me, and I bring up my missing boogie board. We yell at each other. I push him. The push was meant to be one step above a playful shove, but he loses his balance. His head cracks against the Generator from Hell's frame on the way down. I buy a flight out of Puerto Rico (it cost me all my savings). I'm keeping a low profile somewhere in South America now.

Not really.

I do my best to listen. The father looks tired and a little sad. It's hard enough to understand another human being when you both speak the same language, and I realize just how much we don't understand each other. (Puerto Rican Spanish has been tough for me, since many people on the island don't enunciate certain words. For example, "*todo bien*" is just "*to bien.*" But Dominicans put their own flavor on top of that. For instance, if you hear someone from the Dominican Republic say "fabus," they probably mean "facebook.")

"*No entiendo.*" (I don't understand). I say this and he keeps trying to explain, but this time I interrupt. "*Está mejor. Gracias.*" (It's better. Thanks.) I hadn't meant to thank him, but to my surprise, my words ring true.

Approaching the son is more challenging. I wait until he's talking with friends on the sidewalk. He squares his shoulders and raises his chin, but I make my own flow.

I shake hands with him, ever so carefully.

I wish I could say that it ended there with a handshake, but that's not quite the whole truth. After about a week, the neighbors finally run their Generator from Hell to death. They get another generator, a 7500W model instead of the 5000W one. While this new generator is probably safer than the previous model, it somehow manages to be even louder. It's a nonstop jackhammer. I never thought I'd miss the Generator from Hell.

Still, Lilliana and I manage to keep a polite distance from the neighbors. Then, after 66 days of no power... the electricity returns to our building!

The power fades in and out intermittently, but it looks like it'll stick around. The only issue is the power hasn't yet returned to the building that houses our neighbors' business. That shouldn't be our problem, but the dynamic between us and them seems to shift, as if we've done something wrong. My guess is that our neighbors are used to being Haves and can't stand the possibility of being Have-Nots.

One evening, they let the GFH 2.0 rumble out its satanic hymns past 1 in the morning. Lilliana has to get up early the next morning, and she's going insane. When they finally shut the generator off, she goes out to the balcony to complain.

I had always thought that any confrontation would take place between me and the son, but Lilliana proves me wrong. The daughter of the family is in the alleyway screaming at her, and Lilliana is screaming back. I join her on the balcony and watch in silence.

Most of the family, except for the father, is in the street. The shouting dies down, and Lilliana storms back into the apartment. I'm left looking down at them.

I think about how this family tormented us at night, took up our space, and posed a threat to our safety.

And now the daughter wants to scream at us while we're in our home?

I want to convey the past two months to them. Surprisingly, the hate is gone.

"*Mira. Mira. Mira. No tienen respeto. Buenas noches.*" (Look. Look. Look. You have no respect. Good night.)

I close the balcony door and return to my life.

After I go inside, the daughter shrieks like a wounded elephant for minutes on end.

That's no longer my problem.

The next morning, power returned to their building.

SE LEVANTA

#PRSeLevanta

This means "Puerto Rico rises." It bothers me.

At first, I thought it was just because I don't like hashtags. I understand hashtags are useful for tagging topics in the digital world, but that quality of being occasionally useful doesn't automatically earn my trust. For example, I don't particularly like air conditioners, cars, or umbrellas either. Plus, many hashtags are simply misplaced modifiers when you get down to it.

But I see *Puerto Rico se levanta* in other forms without the hashtag, and it still bothers me. I don't know who started the catchphrase, but Puerto Rico's government and US businesses have no qualms about using these words to their advantage. I see it on billboards along the highways and plastered on T-shirts.

#PRSeLevanta

What caused the fall?

"*Puerto Rico no se levanta porque Puerto Rico siempre ha estado de pie.*" (Puerto Rico does not rise because Puerto Rico has always been standing). Residente from the band Calle 13 said that at the 2017 Latin Grammy Awards in Las Vegas. I appreciate his sentiment, but I can't completely agree.

It may not be my place to say so, but Puerto Rico fell long before hurricanes Irma and Maria.

Here's the situation as I understand it:

Puerto Rico is an unincorporated territory of the United States. All legal residents here are considered US citizens, yet they have little to no say about US laws that could affect them. They cannot vote in the US presidential election. They have no one to cast a vote for them in the House of Representatives and Senate. That's basically part of what it means to be an unincorporated territory.

At the same time, the entire population of US unincorporated territories is about four million, and Puerto Rico accounts for the overwhelming majority of this population. Despite the continuous trickle of people leaving for the States, the island has well over three million inhabitants, a higher population than about 20 of the 50 states. Puerto Rico has 78 municipalities, 78 different mayors. You can hang out in parts of San Juan that look like AnywhereTown, USA, then bike a few miles to Loíza and see a different country.

In many ways Puerto Rico feels like its own small country, but it has never been a sovereign nation. The island was a Spanish colony until 1898, when the territory was ceded to the US at the end of the Spanish-American War. And so began a confusing, sometimes unhealthy relationship with the United States of America.

Puerto Rico's $73 billion debt is tied to this bizarre relationship. US lawmakers wanted to modernize Puerto Rico's economy and drive more business and manufacturing to the island. The key to this development was attracting US corporations. What drew those companies to the island? Tax incentives, of course. The plan seemed to work. Throughout much of the twentieth century, the island's standard of living grew and grew.

As this boom continued, a US tax break passed in 1976 coupled with Puerto Rico's own corporate tax code allowed subsidiaries on the island to basically avoid corporate taxes on profits sent back to their parent companies. Even more firms were happy to do business here.

In 1996, the US decided to phase out this tax loophole over the next 10 years, since those advantages were ultimately seen as taking away money from the States and being too favorable for corporations. Companies began leaving the island, and Puerto Rico's economy began to spiral downward in 2006 and has been going that way ever since.

So Puerto Rico's debt is all the United States' fault then, right? Well, there's shortsightedness and incompetence on both sides of the Atlantic. Another advantage that Puerto Rico had going for it was triple-tax-exempt bonds. A bond is basically an IOU that a government can issue when it wants investors to give them money; in return, the government promises to pay investors interest at regular intervals and to repay the bond's original amount after a certain period of time. Triple-tax-exempt meant that investors didn't have to pay federal, state, or local taxes on whatever interest they made. Government bonds are supposed to be low-risk, and the tax perks were irresistible. Many people bought bonds from the Puerto Rican government.

Even while the economy was apparently flourishing, this borrowed money from bonds was being used by the Puerto Rican government to balance its budget. When the US corporations left and the economy took a nosedive in 2006, the government started issuing even more bonds to keep itself afloat. This was probably an act of desperation spurred on by politicians who wanted higher approval ratings. The government was not able to make the interest payments on those ballooning bonds much less pay back the original amount. Puerto Rico's credit rating was downgraded, which resulted in bonds with higher interest rates being issued to keep attracting investors. This snowball effect accounts for most of the $73 billion debt.

To complicate matters further, it's not as if all this debt is owned by some sick Wall Street CEO who can only become aroused while watching the apartment murder scene from *American Psycho*. Residents in all 50 states and in Puerto Rico bought these bonds. If you invest and have a bond mutual fund, there's not an insignificant chance that some of it might include Puerto Rico's ill-fated bonds.

Despite a heavy sales tax of 11.5% in addition to income tax, the Puerto Rican government has been unable to make a dent in this debt. Part of this may be due to inefficient tax collection on the local level, but there's also a dwindling number of taxpayers. Young professionals are fleeing the island, there's a large cash economy with income not being reported, and the remaining aging population pays fewer taxes while requiring more social services.

Oh yeah as an unincorporated territory, Puerto Rico can't follow typical bankruptcy procedures and it must rely heavily on the US government for how it can restructure its debt.

Puerto Rico is between a rock and a – it's screwed.

And now the two big players during the decades that led up to this mess, US corporations and the Puerto Rican government, want to say that Puerto Rico rises? Give me a break.

#PRSeLevanta

How is it rising?

The current status as an unincorporated territory isn't sustainable. It's a toxic relationship. Something has to change, and the two main options that are often presented are statehood and independence.

Statehood: this route could provide some relief for the island. As a state, Puerto Rico could receive more federal funding than it does now and have better tools for handling its debt. There's probably enough support on the island for statehood to work, and a framework already exists for US territories to become states. Still, if every eligible Puerto Rican voted yes for statehood today, there's no guarantee it would happen.

Remember the voting here has no binding effect on the US federal government, so the final decision rests with US Congress. Adding another state to the union where most of the voters lean towards Democrat could be the stuff of nightmares for many members of Congress. Plus, the long-term costs associated with statehood are uncertain at best.

Independence: I think this would be the more exciting option, but there would be a number of difficulties to overcome. As an island, Puerto Rico doesn't have a lot of natural resources that could be used to create typical manufacturing industries. The government could try to offer more tax incentives to attract foreign investment and corporations, but that creation of an artificial economy that can vanish the moment conditions become less favorable was part of the original problem. One alternative could be to focus on a more agrarian economy; this would more closely resemble the Puerto Rican economy from the early twentieth century, before US corporations and manufacturing usurped agriculture.

Puerto Rico has good land and favorable growing conditions, but most of its produce today is imported. There would need to be a massive training program in place for working with the land, and there would need to be a willing workforce. Young, successful people would need to come back from the States and throw their lot in with this endeavor.

For all of its economic woes, Puerto Rico still has a higher standard of living than most of Latin America and the Caribbean. This standard of living would likely drop considerably while the island negotiated its own trade agreements and found its way. There's also that same hurdle that we have with statehood: the US would need to approve Puerto Rico's independence. The island could start a revolution and break away on its own, but that would almost certainly mean years of violence.

Don't forget that the debt still hangs over both options. One way or another, it would have to be addressed.

So...

#¿PRSeLevanta?

I'm worried that those who are already standing tall are using *Puerto Rico se levanta* to lift themselves even higher.

I'm worried that most people on the island who repeat these words are being set up to take another fall.

I'm worried that these words are a feel-good catchphrase that doesn't advocate for real change.

But what about the private citizens rising up to lift up their fellow man? I have met some that have come back to the island (often at their own expense) to help family members, friends, and total strangers with rebuilding efforts. In the States, many people have raised money and supplies to provide aid to hurricane-shattered Puerto Rico. Perhaps you are one of those people.

I think that's beautiful, but that is not Puerto Rico rising.

That's hurricane relief efforts.

Maria was a ferocious storm, but the aftermath shouldn't have been as terrible. People shouldn't have to go without power and clean drinking water for months. They shouldn't have to pay the price for irresponsible actions taken by two governments: one across the sea in which they have no representation, and one right here at home that hasn't worked in their best interests.

Deep-seated problems were made worse by a passing hurricane. Simply fixing Maria's damage isn't going to solve those problems. Presenting #PRSeLevanta as being all about a force of nature and our response to it is another way to accept the status quo.

That's about the extent of my knowledge. I don't know what Puerto Rico should do. I don't know how to answer those questions. All I know is I'm not going to throw around *Puerto Rico se levanta* while the situation proves otherwise.

FROM WHERE HURRICANES COME

We like to think that each hurricane is different. We give them categories 1-5 like that will actually tell us something. We go through the alphabet for names, A to Z, male to female, then back again. We try to make each big bad storm all about our tiny but somehow still important struggles. That's okay. It's not true, but that's okay.

It's not true because each hurricane is really the same. I'm talking about the eye of each hurricane. In the center, past the irises and Irmas, smack-dab in the pupil, is an Atlantian passing through our world.

Yes, an Atlantian from the Lost City of Atlantis. No, Atlantis didn't sink or go extinct. The city simply moved on, beyond, and along but not really up or down or around... it's difficult to give a direction to something advancing past human. Let's just say that Atlantians inhabit a different dimension – dimensions, really.

Sometimes, one comes back to Earth to get in touch with its roots.

That's why we have hurricanes...

Don't laugh – traveling between dimensions is serious business. If you tried to do it, you'd probably start an interstellar war or at least misplace Venus, but an Atlantian only makes a hurricane.

Plus, there are benefits to having the occasional Atlantian visit your world. Have you ever encountered someone who wears way too much cologne? You can smell them two streets down before you see them. Atlantians are like that, except with power and knowledge instead of cologne. They ooze ideas and we hang onto their coattails after each storm.

Here's a fun fact: Even though Maria has knocked out the Wi-Fi, we wouldn't even have Wi-Fi if it weren't for this one hurricane back in the 90s.

Now, most Atlantians are fairly decent at heart, but the one who tried to poke its head through Maria's eye over Puerto Rico wasn't so great. This Atlantian used to be the director of the Universe Conservation League, which is a little like our own Environmental Protection Agency. The UCL does stuff like preserving parallel realities and freeing moon whales that have become quantum entangled. Normally it's a good agency, but this director was pretending to conserve dimensions while stealing them instead. Embezzling. Emdimensionalizing.

What was his name?

It was Snibubububububububububrrrkumkop.

Can it be shorter?

Yeah, his friends called him Snibu, although anyone who wanted to be friends with the guy was probably a jerk. Anyway, Snibu was stealing dimensions as the director of the UCL, but he finally got caught. He didn't want to give up all that emdimensionalized merchandise, so he needed to find a sort of offshore bank account.

That's why he came to Puerto Rico through Hurricane Maria: He wanted to dump all those dimensions here.

When someone says, "Hey, that added another

dimension to my life," it's usually a positive – but dimensions with an 'S' spinning through our lives?

The world as we know it would cease to exist.

We saw the beginnings of that when sailboats walked on land and sheet metal sailed through air, but it could've been worse.

Our voices, our feet, our faces could've gotten so jumbled up that our ability to communicate, to keep moving forward, to recognize each other as human beings could've been consumed by chaos.

All that to enrich one Atlantian.

Luckily, entering our world through the eye of a hurricane requires intense concentration. And there was at least one voice calling out despite the whirlwinds. That voice must've been enough to interrupt Snibu as he was poking his Atlantian snout out through the Atlantic, enough to keep him from making that final transaction over Puerto Rico.

I heard that voice still calling when I went to check out the damage after the eye of Maria had left San Juan.

A zinc roof from the neighboring apartment building had fallen on and collapsed the roof of our building's laundry room, after narrowly missing a couple of leaky propane tanks that had been left outside our bathroom window by a forgetful business owner. The voice came from that wreckage:

Co

Co-Qui

Co-Qui

Yes! It was that voice that had distracted Snibu and kept Maria from turning the island completely upside-down. It was the single Coqui frog that we share with the neighboring apartment building. In better weather, I would mimic its call. A neighbor from the other building would do the same. I suspect our Coqui sometimes took a break, letting me and the unseen neighbor call out to each other in a language we didn't really understand.

On that day after Maria, I saw our Coqui for the first time. It was simply a small, light-brown frog that's native to Puerto Rico. A frog whose throat and stomach undulated while it chirped its name.

In the weeks after Maria, our Coqui fell silent. As for the power and knowledge left behind by an Atlantian in the wake of a hurricane, I don't know but... *mucha gente está afuera.*

I see more people walking dogs they forgot they had. I wait in lines with neighbors I never knew existed. My girlfriend and I have romantic candle-lit dinners after she discovers that the candles can be used to heat our soup. Strangest of all to me, I stop wasting time and actually finish something.

The Coqui won't stay silent forever. And when they make their call again, I hope that we don't shut ourselves inside, tune them out, and return to our old ways.

I hope their call sounds like a rediscovery, like leftover power and knowledge from the lost city of Atlantis echoing across our island.

BONUS STORIES FOR READERS

Looks like you've reached the end of the book. It's time to say goodbye, but let's not make it awkward. Seriously, you're making me uncomfortable. Okay I'm just going to let myself out while you read these two stories:

***

NEW BEGINNINGS
For Susan

There is a man who knows the future. He is not a god – he just happens to possess the all-see'ums, a pair of goggles capable of viewing all to come.

So how do you steal the all-see'ums from that man when he knows what you're going to do before you do it?

That's the question that Susan must answer. A difficult question because she does not believe the future exists. For Susan, everything takes place in the present. This is Susan's story, so we must do our best to stay in the present.

Susan's a professional thief, so at least she has that going for her. But everything else about this job is all wrong. Art is her specialty, and she never fools around with so-called magical items if she can help it. Stealing stuff like the all-see'ums carries too many liabilities: curses, hexes, and maledictions to name a few.

Yeah, art is her specialty, but art is what gets Susan into this mess. Unbeknownst to Susan, the last stolen painting belongs to one Doña Chica.

Collecting art is a lucrative pastime for the mob. Laundered money and art get along just fine. The Doña wants her painting to go to auction and turn a few million into legitimate funds. When someone like Susan comes along, steals the painting, and hurts careful plans, the Doña is not pleased.

"You don't have our money or the painting? How about we murder you right now? You don't want to be murdered? How about you get those all-see'ums, wrap them up real nice, and deliver them to the Doña? We are watching."

That is pretty much the extent of the conversation when the Doña's affiliates bribe and beat their way back to Susan. So, like it or not, Susan needs to trick a man who can see the future into parting with his most prized possession.

That man's name is Stanley Cooper, and he resides where most people who think they know how to play the future go. He resides in that improbable city called Las Vegas.

All Susan has is the present. She must try to imagine the future from Cooper's perspective.

How much of an imaginary future can that man see? Is he able to see only the events that directly affect him, or can he view anything, like the life and times of a chicken that's going to be born in Cambodia next February? Susan decides that Cooper can only see a limited future that involves him, since she doesn't have time to mess around with the infinite.

Here is Susan's final plan for retrieving the all-see'ums:

*She needs five Susans, including herself. The others are lookalikes: carefully trained, highly paid, and not risk-averse.
*Each Susan travels to Las Vegas via a different route.
*Each Susan crosses paths multiple times on the way to Vegas.
*Each Susan has a pair of magnetic jogging goggles, which resemble Cooper's all-see'um goggles.
*Each lookalike Susan puts on her lookalike goggles and gets Cooper's attention in her own way, one after the other on the same day.
*The real Susan grabs the real all-see'ums in the middle of this pandemonium.

If Cooper is watching the future that Susan has in store for him, he sees five identical women wearing what may be his all-see'ums. He sees five thieves running in five different directions at five different times to five different places. Susan likes her odds.

At the Nashville airport, Susan meets one of her lookalikes and passes her the ticket for a connecting flight to Las Vegas. The real Susan leaves the airport and has time to kill before her next move. She heads to Nudie's Honky Tonk, which is billed as the longest bar in Nashville.

The bar in Nudie's Honky Tonk is very long, and Susan is mildly impressed. She walks to the middle and plans to order a piña colada no rum, her favorite drink. Just as she gets the bartender's attention, a little man cuts in front of her, even though there is at least twenty feet of empty bar on either side. This man is shaped like a bowling pin. He wears a white polyester suit and an alabaster cowboy hat that is much too big.

"Two piña coladas no rum. On the double, or take your time. What will be, will be," he says to the bartender then turns toward Susan. Two blue lenses glitter under the shade of his hat. "Hi Susan. I'm going to enjoy this conversation."

Susan's plan is not going as planned. This man with the blue lenses, the all-see'ums wrapped around his face, is Stanley Cooper. She takes a seat at the longest bar in Nashville, and Cooper does the same. They sit in silence until the piña coladas arrive.

"So, aren't you going to ask me?" Cooper says.

"Ask you what?" Susan doesn't like it when a man who can supposedly see the future asks her a question.

"Is the future predetermined, or is it changeable? Do I see probabilities or timelines set in stone?"

"That's two questions, and it looks like you just asked them," Susan says. She isn't going to play games with Cooper.

"Lighten up Susan. I see many more piña coladas in your future." Cooper sips his and grimaces. "I knew I wasn't going to like that."

"Listen, I don't want your all-see'ums. I'm coming after them because I don't have a choice."

"It wasn't a bad plan, but I only saw four Susans running around Las Vegas. I'm looking forward to seeing it again, but I really wanted to meet the fifth one."

"How do I know you're the real Stanley Cooper?" All this talk of lookalikes has Susan wondering.

"Hmmm... say anything you please. I'll say it with you. 3, 2, 1. Go."

"Spliff-o-matic-pro-chromatic-autosomatic-take-no-static," they say in unison.

"By the way, that connecting flight to Vegas that you skipped. That plane is going to crash in about 37 minutes."

"Oh my God."

"Sorry, the plane and your double will be fine... probably. Simply trying to lighten the conversation."

"Cut the shit Cooper."

"Don't curse, Susan. You're better than that."

"I need you tell me what's going to happen." Susan toys with the cherry in her drink. She tells herself that if the cherry sinks, either Cooper or Doña Chica is going to kill her. If the cherry floats, she is fine in the present. The future doesn't exist.

"A lot is going to happen. Too much. But you don't have to worry about that. To be honest, I thought about plucking your thread out of the tapestry of time. Only a little snip, and bye-bye Susan while the pattern continues, but then I thought about what you had to offer me."

"Is this the part where you're going to tell me your evil plan?"

"Sure. Here's what's going to happen. I'm going to give you the all-see'ums."

"Are you drunk? You give them to me, and I deliver them to Doña Chica? Just like that?"

"Keep up Susan. You don't want to deliver the all-see'ums to Doña Chica. You think she'll want someone around who will know she has them?"

"I don't want to keep them. I don't even believe in the future." Susan notices that Nudie's Honky Tonk is starting to fill up with more people. How many of them are keeping eyes on her for Doña Chica?

"I know. That's why I'm giving them to you."

"What's in it for you, Cooper?"

"Imagine knowing the time, place, and manner of your death. No, let's back it up a bit. Imagine knowing the day when your wife of 27 years will stop loving you. No, even smaller. Imagine knowing what you're going to have for lunch for the rest of your life. I don't even enjoy food anymore."

"Then you can't change the future with your fancy goggles?"

"Not exactly. I think Tolstoy says it best in the

second epilogue in *War and Peace*: 'Freedom is the thing examined. Inevitability is what examines. Freedom is the content. Inevitability is the form.'"

"I haven't read that one."

"Me neither, but I've already seen that I am going to read it. But let's go back to the original question: is the future changeable?"

"You're saying it can be changed a little bit."

"What I'm saying, Susan, is that I see a future where I may one day be surprised."

"Great. You're going to unload the all-see'ums on me, and I get to deal with Doña Chica while you go on some philosophical quest."

"How many pairs of eyes do you think Doña Chica has on you right now?" Cooper glances at the country music band setting up on stage. "Oh my, you think that gee-tar player over yonder is working for her? Picture this – there are four Susan lookalikes flying all across the country right now. I'd say those eyes are spread pretty thin. In fact, I'd go so far as to say that there's just one pair of eyes waiting outside in a black SUV. When the band begins to play, that one watcher will receive an upsetting phone call from his mistress."

Before Susan can reply, Cooper unclips the all-see'ums and tosses them on the bar in front of her drink. He takes off his alabaster cowboy hat and places it over the goggles. Cooper's eyes are naked and glistening. He looks like the sort of guy who would be happy to trade home improvement tips with you at the hardware store.

"Thanks Susan. Remember when the band starts to play that's your cue." Cooper takes off into the crowd, his bald white pin head vanishing behind denim-clad shoulders.

When the honky tonk band opens up, the dance floor is packed. A line dance, with heavy boot heels clicking and clacking against the hardwood floor, takes shape.

Susan's plan is less complicated this time. She takes the all-see'ums out and tosses them ever so smoothly onto that dance floor amid the stomping heels.

Click. Clash. Clack. Crack. No more future.

She puts on Cooper's hat and pulls the brim down low. On the way out of Nudie's Honky Tonk she grabs a jacket from a bar stool. There's a black SUV with out-of-state plates in the parking lot. The driver is having a heated discussion on his cell phone and doesn't once look her way.

No one follows her.

Susan isn't going to say that she all of sudden believes in the future. But just in that moment walking down Nashville's streets with her new cowboy hat and jacket, she is also somehow on a beach making a painting instead of stealing it. And of course, there is a piña colada with no rum close at hand.

***

HOPE
For Kelley

Before Captain Kelley tore through our azure skies, life on Pnub was all about rocks, rocks, and more rocks. Mining, trading, and collecting rocks was very important. The best people on Pnub were the ones who owned the best rocks, of course.

After she landed, Captain Kelley stole the best rocks from the best people and gave their rocks to the worst people. Then, when the worst people started acting like the best people, the Captain took the best rocks away from everyone! It was a very confusing time for the people of Pnub.

We don't know where Captain Kelley came from or why she did this to us. All we know is that she was terrible. She once made Cobalt Pete cry in front of everyone by calling his rocks worthless. Everyone knew that Cobalt Pete had the best of the best rocks.

The people of Pnub all agreed that capturing Captain Kelley would put a stop to this madness.

That was easier said than done. Captain Kelley's ship was very fast. We tried to follow her in the tugboats used to haul rocks, but those were too slow.

We never would've been able to catch her that way.

Finally, Sandstone Jill got a really strange idea. What if we dumped the rocks off the tugboats to make them lighter? We tried it, and the tugboats traveled higher up into the sky than they ever had before. But Captain Kelley soared even higher, staying just out of reach.

Hmmm... what if we made tugboats that weren't designed to carry rocks at all? We made the tugboats smaller, sleeker, and speedier. Somewhere along the way, we stopped calling them tugboats and starting calling them ships.

Some of us followed Captain Kelley all the way up to Pnub's moons. These moons had interesting rocks that couldn't be found down on the planet. We began mining the moon rocks, but Captain Kelley wouldn't stop bothering us.

She said that she had the best of all rocks, and that we couldn't have this rock because we were too slow and stupid. Then, she took off into the skies and flew to another planet beyond Pnub's moons. We experimented with different moon rocks until we found one that could make our ships go very fast. Some of us chased after Captain Kelley and made it to the next planet.

After careful consideration, we decided to call this planet Pnub II.

Pnub II had rocks, but it had a lot of other things too. It had things that went squawk and things that glowed in the night and things that grew ever taller each year while giving us shade from the sun. And those were just some of the things other than rocks that we found. This too was a very confusing time for the people of Pnub II.

And Captain Kelley still wouldn't leave us alone. She no longer claimed to have the best of all rocks. Instead, she said that she had something that was better than the best of all rocks. The next time she took off, some of us followed her to the next planet.

Rocks are sometimes still important, but life for the people of Pnub, Pnub's moons, Pnub II, and the planets beyond is no longer all about rocks.

We haven't seen Captain Kelley in quite some time, but we keep searching for new worlds. We aren't sure why.

It can't be for greed. We have more than we ever could have imagined.

It can't be for revenge. Captain Kelley was awful, but she never hurt our people.

This thing makes us want to go a little farther, to find something a little better, to keep trying year after year. We don't yet have a name for it.

Perhaps when we find that thing that Captain Kelley promised us, that thing that is better than the best of all rocks, we will know what to call it.

Robert Egan lives in San Juan but wants to be everywhere and nowhere at the same time. He's also lived in Honolulu, Chicago, Austin, and Belgrade. This book started with an improvised tale told during one of Puerto Rico's many blackouts. Learn more about the inspiration behind this book at RobertEganBooks.com

Author Photography by Estuardo Linde

Made in the USA
San Bernardino, CA
24 June 2019